REPTILES & AMPHIBIANS

POISONOUS SNAKES

Brenda Ralph Lewis

GARETH**STEVENS**

GS

PUBLISHING

A Member of the WRC Media Family of Companies

Please visit our web site at: **www.garethstevens.com**
For a free color catalog describing Gareth Stevens Publishing's
list of high-quality books and multimedia programs,
call 1-800-542-2595 (USA) or 1-800-387-3178 (Canada).
Gareth Stevens Publishing's fax: (414) 332-3567.

Library of Congress Cataloging-in-Publication Data

Lewis, Brenda Ralph.
 Poisonous snakes / Brenda Ralph Lewis. — North American ed.
  p. cm. — (Nature's monsters: Reptiles & amphibians)
 Includes bibliographical references and index.
 ISBN 0-8368-6174-4 (lib. bdg.)
 1. Poisonous snakes—Juvenile literature. I. Title. II. Series.
 QL666.O6L723   2006
 597.96′165—dc22   2005054174

This North American edition first published in 2006 by
Gareth Stevens Publishing
A Member of the WRC Media Family of Companies
330 West Olive Street, Suite 100
Milwaukee, WI 53212 USA

Original edition and illustrations copyright © 2006 by International Masters Publishers AB.
Produced by Amber Books Ltd., Bradley's Close, 74–77 White Lion Street, London N1 9PF, U.K.

Project editor: Michael Spilling
Design: Joe Conneally

Gareth Stevens editorial direction: Valerie J. Weber
Gareth Stevens art direction: Tammy West
Gareth Stevens production: Jessica Morris

Printed in the United States of America

1 2 3 4 5 6 7 8 9 10 09 08 07 06

Contents

Continents of the World

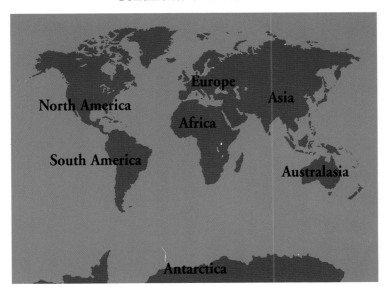

The world is divided into seven continents — North America, South America, Europe, Africa, Asia, Australasia, and Antarctica. In this book, the area where each animal lives is shown in red, while all land is shown in green.

Words that appear in the glossary are printed in **boldface** type the first time they occur in the text.

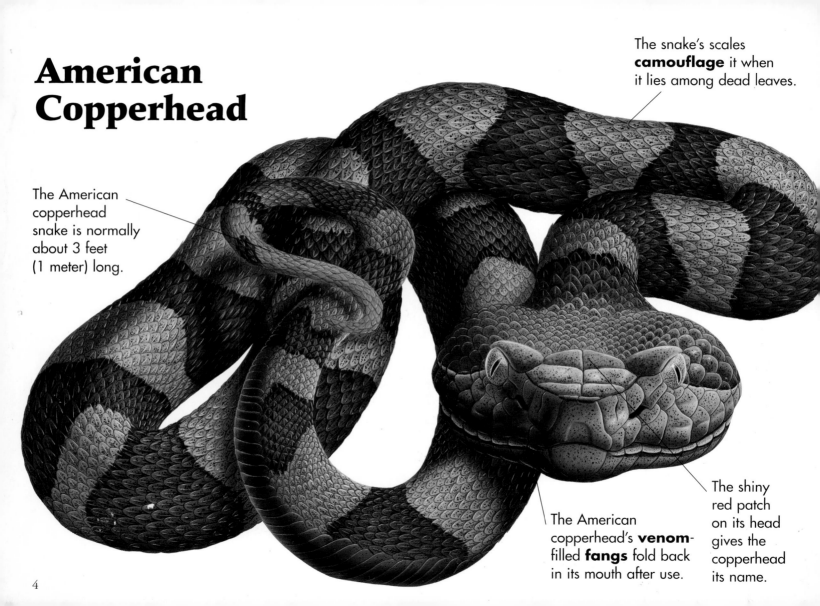

American Copperhead

The snake's scales **camouflage** it when it lies among dead leaves.

The American copperhead snake is normally about 3 feet (1 meter) long.

The American copperhead's **venom**-filled **fangs** fold back in its mouth after use.

The shiny red patch on its head gives the copperhead its name.

The American copperhead snake is usually shy. The snake rarely attacks first. If disturbed or hurt, however, it will react violently and strike its attacker.

Size

1 The American copperhead snake can easily disguise itself. It may look like dead leaves lying on the forest floor. It might curl itself into a "pancake" shape and lie completely still.

2 If the snake is directly attacked, it will fight back. Fortunately for the attacker, an American copperhead doesn't usually produce more than 1 grain (65 milligrams) of venom. Although this man suffers a bad bite, it will probably not be **lethal**. The fangs may leave behind some nasty **scars**.

Where in the World

Three of the ten species of copperheads live in the eastern United States. The others are found in Asia, including Okinawa Island in Japan and the Himalaya Mountains.

Water Moccasin

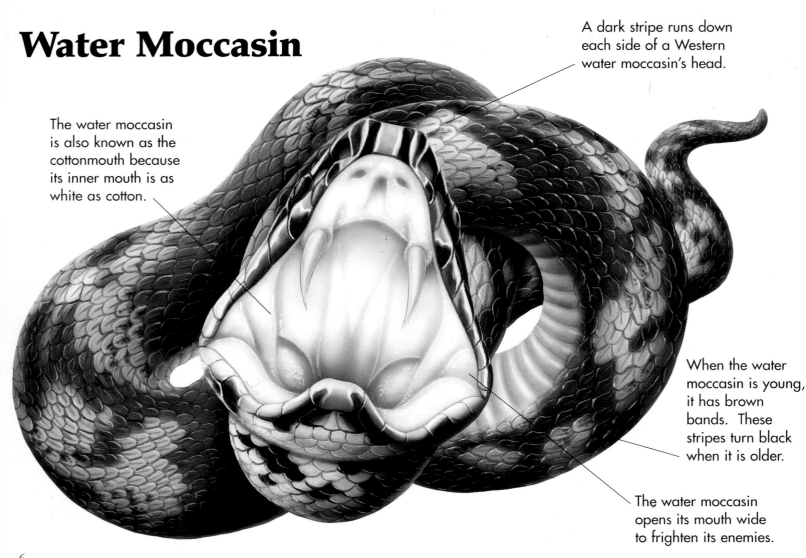

A dark stripe runs down each side of a Western water moccasin's head.

The water moccasin is also known as the cottonmouth because its inner mouth is as white as cotton.

When the water moccasin is young, it has brown bands. These stripes turn black when it is older.

The water moccasin opens its mouth wide to frighten its enemies.

The water moccasin lives in or near ponds, **bayous**, and other waterways. It is called the water moccasin because of its silent way of sneaking up on its **prey**.

Size

1 The two men paddling their canoe through a Florida bayou do not realize how fast the water moccasin snake can strike when it is disturbed.

2 Suddenly, the water moccasin leaps up and sinks its long fangs into the man's wrist. The length of its fangs allows the snake to hang on, no matter how hard its victim tries to shake it off.

3 The snake **injects** its venom, giving the man a powerful dose of poison. It may kill him.

Where in the World

Water moccasins live along the Atlantic coast of North America and the Gulf of Mexico. They live in water **habitats** stretching from southern Virginia to Florida and also live in Texas, Oklahoma, and Illinois.

Puff Adder

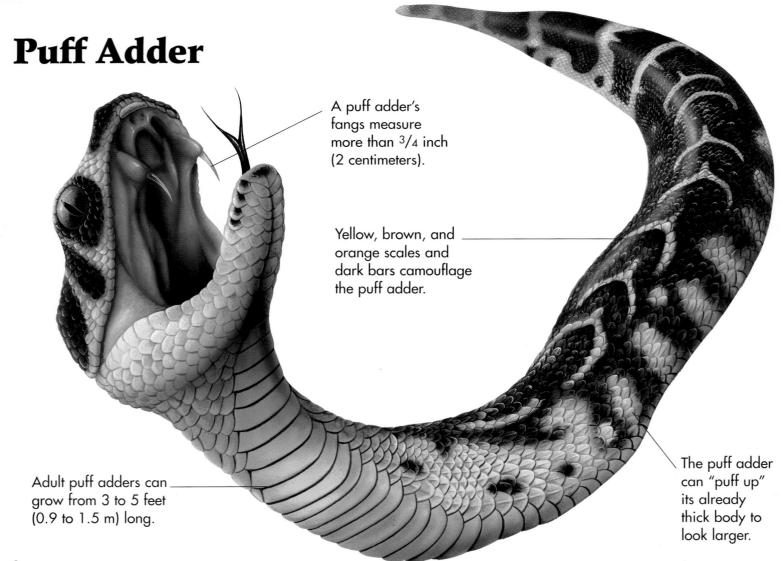

A puff adder's fangs measure more than 3/4 inch (2 centimeters).

Yellow, brown, and orange scales and dark bars camouflage the puff adder.

Adult puff adders can grow from 3 to 5 feet (0.9 to 1.5 m) long.

The puff adder can "puff up" its already thick body to look larger.

Like other vipers, the puff adder has very **flexible** jawbones, which allow it to open its mouth wide to swallow its prey whole.

Puff adders like to lie around in the heat of the day. Often they do not bother to hunt for their food but eat whatever prey passes by.

1 Puff adders do not waste venom on small creatures, such as frogs or rats, or open their mouths wide to take them in. The snakes just swallow them whole while they are still alive.

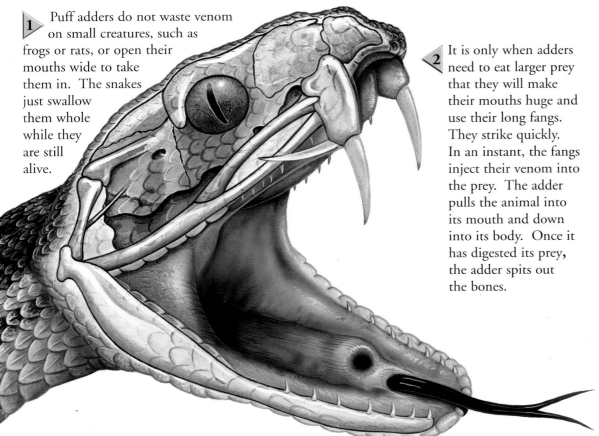

2 It is only when adders need to eat larger prey that they will make their mouths huge and use their long fangs. They strike quickly. In an instant, the fangs inject their venom into the prey. The adder pulls the animal into its mouth and down into its body. Once it has digested its prey, the adder spits out the bones.

Where in the World

Puff adders can be found in most of the African **continent**. They also live in the Middle East, especially in the lowlands of Saudi Arabia.

Gaboon Viper

A stripe runs down the middle of the gaboon viper's head.

The gaboon viper has the longest fangs of any snake in the world — almost 2 inches (5 cm).

A gaboon viper's camouflage comes from its light and dark brown coloring.

The viper's body measures up to 18 inches (45 cm) round and 6 feet, 6 inches (2 m) long.

10

The only way the toothless gaboon viper can take in its food is to open its mouth very wide. The viper uses its powerful muscles to push its prey down into its stomach.

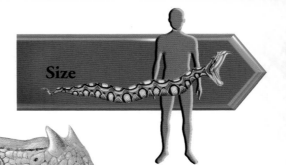

Size

1 When a hungry gaboon viper first opens its mouth, it shows only the tips of its hollow fangs.

Did You Know?

Although it is rare for humans to be bitten, a gaboon viper's venom is so **toxic** that a single dose could kill ten people.

3 The viper pushes its fangs into its prey and injects a huge dose of venom. All the snake has to do now is wait for its prey to die before swallowing it.

2 As the snake leaps toward its prey, its mouth stretches very wide, and its fangs slide out of their **sheaths** into the attack position.

Where in the World

Gaboon vipers live in the forests of central and eastern Africa between southern Sudan and **Zululand** in South Africa. Their habitats have been invaded by hunters who kill them for their meat.

11

Fer-De-Lance

The fer-de-lance (fer-duh-LANTS) keeps its venom in a large **gland** behind its eyes.

The snake's head is triangular and pointed, like a lance or spear-head. That is how it got its name — *fer-de-lance* means "spear" in French.

The fer-de-lance's **pit organ**, located between its eyes and nostrils, can **detect** prey.

The snake's long, curved fangs are inside the top of its mouth.

The golden lancehead, the most deadly fer-de-lance of all, inhabits Quemada Grande island in Brazil. There, the golden lancehead **breeds** in great numbers.

1 A fisherman has brought his boat to Quemada Grande to pick bananas. As he walks through the forest, he disturbs a golden lancehead, which bites his leg. Frightened, he staggers back to his boat. More lanceheads bite him on the way.

2 In great pain, the fisherman reaches the boat. He cuts the snake bites and tries to suck out the poison, but it is no use. He soon falls **unconscious**.

Size

Where in the World

The most numerous fer-de-lance, called "common lanceheads," live in the jungles of Central and South America from southern Mexico to central Brazil.

Asian Pit Viper

The Asian pit viper has eyes that face forward rather than sideways like most other snakes.

The Asian pit viper's long, thin, **forked tongue** can detect smells.

The snake moves along by **alternately** stretching and **contracting** its belly scales.

Tree-dwelling Asian pit vipers use their strong tails to hang from branches.

In cooler weather, pit vipers in Sri Lanka hunt for their food by day. They like to wait in long grass and bushes to ambush their prey — usually small animals, such as frogs, rats, and mice.

1 A woman picks tea leaves on a Sri Lankan plantation and throws them into the basket she carries on her back. The pit viper on the other side of the tea bush is the same color as the leaves. The woman does not notice it.

Where in the World

Asian pit vipers live in India, Nepal, eastern China, Japan, Bangladesh, Myanmar, Thailand, Cambodia, Laos, Vietnam, Indonesia, and Malaysia. They are also known as Malayan pit vipers.

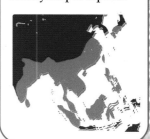

2 As the tea picker moves closer, the bush starts shaking. Scared, the snake jumps up and bites her on the wrist. She screams loudly. If she receives medical aid quickly, she will live.

Desert Horned Viper

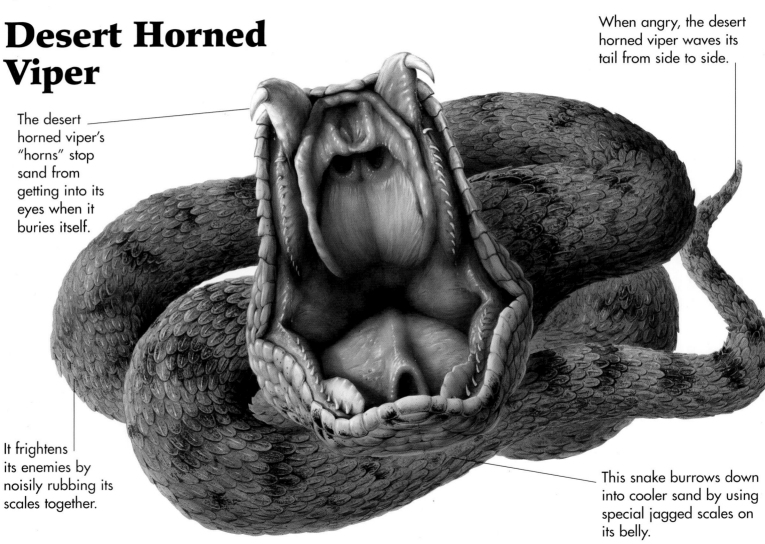

When angry, the desert horned viper waves its tail from side to side.

The desert horned viper's "horns" stop sand from getting into its eyes when it buries itself.

It frightens its enemies by noisily rubbing its scales together.

This snake burrows down into cooler sand by using special jagged scales on its belly.

The desert horned viper hides from the Sun's heat by burrowing into the sand. In a stony desert, it hides beneath a rock. It cannot be seen easily.

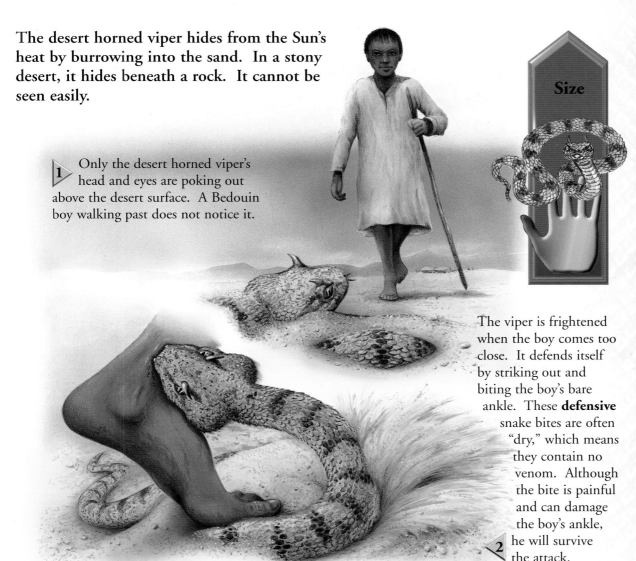

1 ▷ Only the desert horned viper's head and eyes are poking out above the desert surface. A Bedouin boy walking past does not notice it.

The viper is frightened when the boy comes too close. It defends itself by striking out and biting the boy's bare ankle. These **defensive** snake bites are often "dry," which means they contain no venom. Although the bite is painful and can damage the boy's ankle, he will survive the attack. **2** ◁

Size

The desert horned viper is also called a "sidewinder" because of the way it moves across the desert. It throws its body sideways over and over again at high speed.

Where in the World

The desert horned viper lives in deserts throughout North Africa, from Mauritania and Morocco in the west to Egypt in the east — right across the vast Sahara Desert.

Black Mamba

The mamba's mouth stretches wide enough to swallow a small animal whole.

This snake gets its name from the purple-black skin inside its mouth.

The black mamba, the world's deadliest snake, has a coffin-shaped head.

The black mamba's belly has big scales to help it grip the ground when moving.

The black mamba is 14 feet (4.3 m) long and can move at 12 miles (19 kilometers) per hour. It is terrifying if it is disturbed and will attack to defend itself.

Size

1 Although the black mamba lives in Africa, it does not like a lot of heat and often hides from the Sun. A **termite mound** gives it the shade it needs.

2 Four boys playing nearby kick their ball close to the mound, and one of them comes over to get it back. The black mamba is frightened. It defends itself by rising up off the ground, opening its mouth, and shaking its head. The boy runs off in fear.

Where in the World

The black mamba lives in eastern and southern Africa — from Zaire in central Africa to South Africa in the south.

King Cobra

When angry, the king cobra stretches out the "hood" on its neck.

The king cobra finds food smells by "tasting" the air with its tongue.

The king cobra cannot chew its food. Instead it swallows its prey whole.

At 18 feet (5.5 m), the king cobra is the world's longest poisonous snake.

Female king cobras fiercely defend their nests and attack anyone who approaches them. The patch of ground in the forest where a young boy arrives to plant seeds is dangerously close to a king cobra's nest.

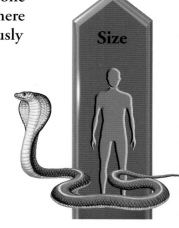

Size

Did You Know?

King cobras are the only snakes to build nests. They have two levels. The female lays about forty eggs on the first and waits on the second for the babies to hatch out of their eggs.

Where in the World

Most cobras live in Africa, but the king cobra is found in Asia. King cobras are common in Malaysia and in India, where they kill hundreds of people every year.

1 This female king cobra rears up in front of the boy. She hisses, spreads out her "hood," and sways from side to side, trying to scare him. The boy is in terrible danger because the cobra can move like lightning and kill with a single bite. Unless this boy is lucky and can escape, the female's fangs will **paralyze** him and stop both his breathing and his heart.

21

Ringhals Cobra

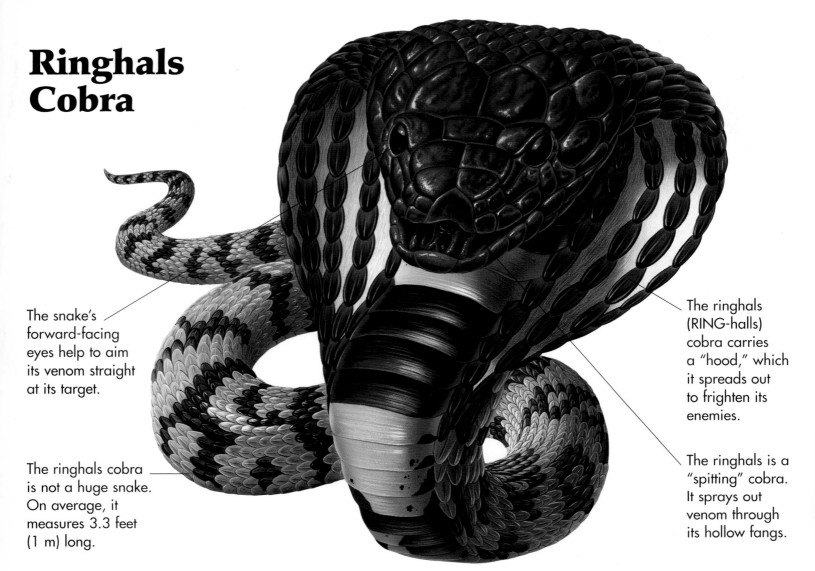

The snake's forward-facing eyes help to aim its venom straight at its target.

The ringhals cobra is not a huge snake. On average, it measures 3.3 feet (1 m) long.

The ringhals (RING-halls) cobra carries a "hood," which it spreads out to frighten its enemies.

The ringhals is a "spitting" cobra. It sprays out venom through its hollow fangs.

Ringhals cobras will pretend to be dead if they think they are in danger. If disturbed or frightened, however, they will fight to defend themselves.

1 A ringhals lies in the sun. A boy approaches, carrying a stick. The cobra is on open ground with nowhere to hide. It pretends to be dead. It rolls on its back, opens its mouth, and lets its tongue hang out.

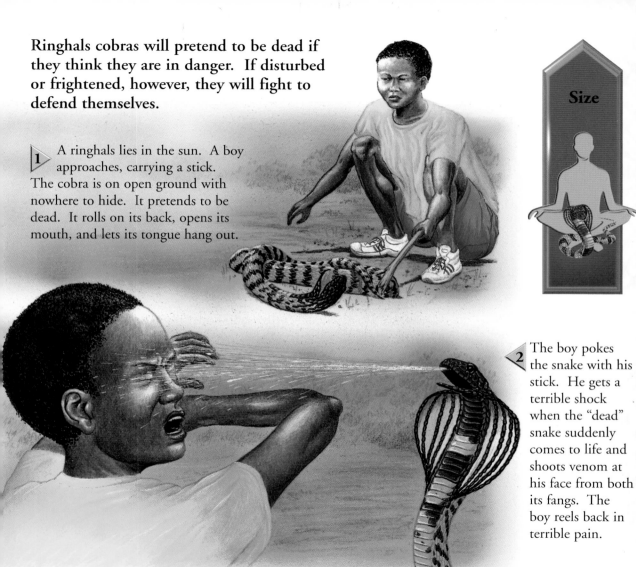

Size

Did You Know?

The name *ringhals,* meaning "ring neck," comes from the Afrikaans language spoken in South Africa. The ringhals cobra has one or more pale bands around its neck.

2 The boy pokes the snake with his stick. He gets a terrible shock when the "dead" snake suddenly comes to life and shoots venom at his face from both its fangs. The boy reels back in terrible pain.

Where in the World

Ringhals cobras are found in eastern South Africa and in the mountainous country in eastern Zimbabwe. They can live at altitudes as high as 8,200 feet (2,500 m).

Tiger Snake

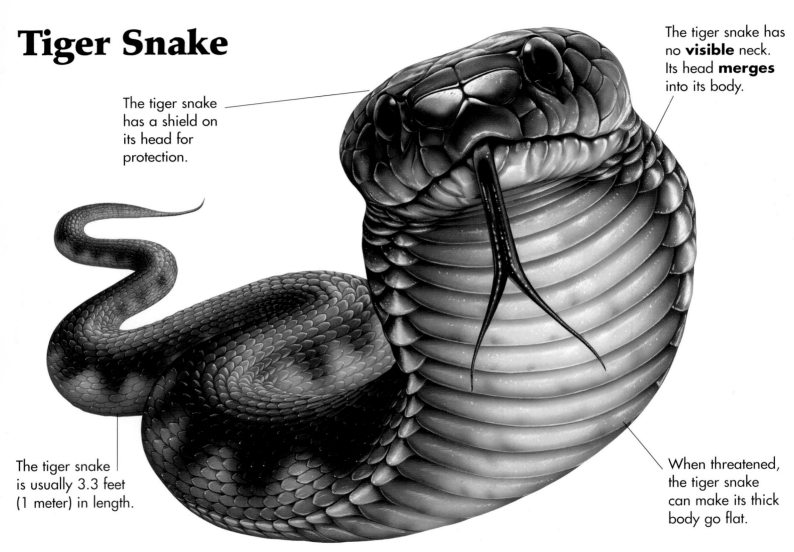

The tiger snake has a shield on its head for protection.

The tiger snake has no **visible** neck. Its head **merges** into its body.

The tiger snake is usually 3.3 feet (1 meter) in length.

When threatened, the tiger snake can make its thick body go flat.

Before it attacks, a tiger snake makes its neck flat and starts hissing. The bite of a tiger snake always kills if the victim cannot get **antivenin** aid.

Size

1 In the Australian bush, a boy accidentally steps on a tiger snake lying nearby. The tiger snake becomes angry and sinks its fangs into the boy's leg. People have compared this snake bite to the bite of a bulldog.

2 The tiger snake may inject only 0.5 grains (32 mg) of venom into its victim. This is one of the most powerful of all venoms, however. It contains twelve or more **toxins**, which soon destroy nerves, blood, and muscles.

Where in the World

Tiger snakes are Australian. They live in the states of Victoria, New South Wales, Queensland, and South Australia. Many people live there, and many suffer deadly tiger snake bites.

Taipan Snake

The taipan (TIE-pan) has the world's deadliest venom, with a bite fifty times more toxic than a cobra's.

The taipan is a long snake, often growing to more than 8 feet (2.4 m).

Openings in the mouth, called **Jacobson's organs**, identify smells detected by the tongue.

The taipan belongs to the family of snakes that have fixed fangs in their mouths.

Long sharp fangs hang from the top of the taipan's mouth. Few snakes have sharper fangs than the taipans'.

1 A man walking in a region of Northern Australia has put on good, strong leather boots with thick socks underneath. Walking along a track, the man does not see the snake. Suddenly, it jumps up with its mouth wide open.

2 Moments later, the taipan has sunk its fangs straight through the thick leather boots. Blood soon flows from the man's ankle.

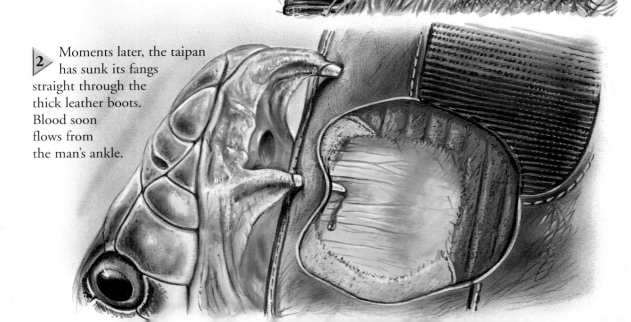

Size

The name *taipan*, or *dhyban* in the Wikmunkan language, comes from an Australian **Aboriginal myth**. The story tells of a serpent so huge that it stretches across the sky like a rainbow.

Where in the World

Taipans live in New Guinea and in Queensland and the Northern Territory in Australia. There is also an **inland** taipan living in a remote area of central Australia.

Bush Viper

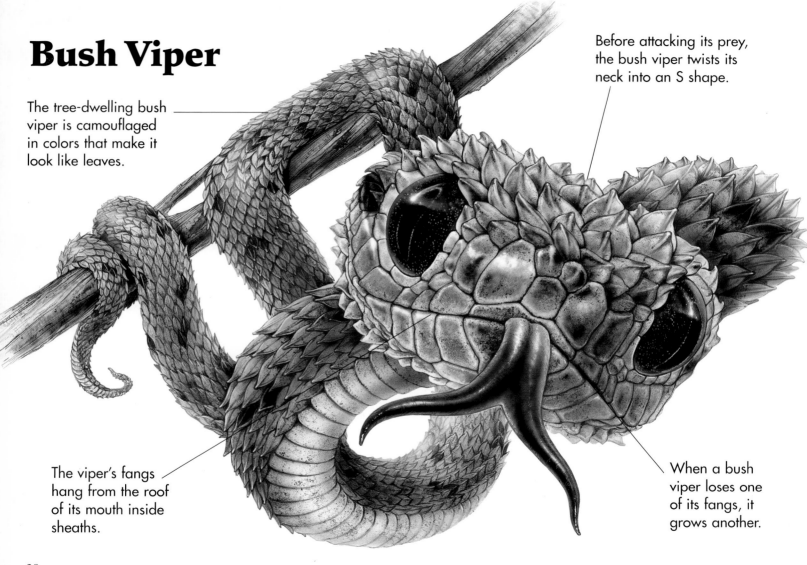

The tree-dwelling bush viper is camouflaged in colors that make it look like leaves.

Before attacking its prey, the bush viper twists its neck into an S shape.

The viper's fangs hang from the roof of its mouth inside sheaths.

When a bush viper loses one of its fangs, it grows another.

Bush vipers can climb trees and balance themselves on the branches. Although they have strong tails to grip a branch, they sometimes lose their balance and fall from the tree.

Size

African hunters once tied vipers together in a long line. The line could trip up animals as large as a buffalo, so that the hunters could capture and kill them.

1 Bush vipers are small snakes, around 30 inches (76 cm) long. They eat small prey, such as lizards, rats, slugs, snails, and birds. The vipers can find lizards up in the trees and creep up on them.

2 Before the viper can reach this lizard, it loses its balance, falling from the branch and onto a man passing below.

3 Frightened by the fall, the snake coils its neck into an S shape, signaling that it is going to strike. The viper soon sinks its fangs into the man's shoulder.

Where in the World

Bush vipers live in central Africa. They can be found in forested areas from Guinea in the west to Mozambique in the east. Today, loggers and house builders threaten their natural habitat.

Glossary

Aboriginal — describing the first people to live in Australia, the Aborigines

alternately — one after the other

antivenin — a drug that cures the effects of snake poison

bayous — marshy areas next to a river or lake

breeds — makes baby animals

camouflage — to disguise or hide

continent — one of the great landmasses on Earth — Africa, North America, South America, Antarctica, Asia, Australasia, and Europe

contracting — pulling in to make smaller

defensive — meant to prevent an attack

detect — to find

digest — to break down food into simpler forms to be used by the body

endangered — to be in danger of dying out altogether

fangs — a snake's long teeth, which often contain poison

flexible — able to bend easily without breaking

forked tongue — a tongue split into two parts at the end

gland — a part of the body that makes special chemicals needed for the body to work properly

habitats — places where animals live

injects — forces fluid into a body

inland — away from the coast

Jacobson's organs — a pair of small tubes inside the throat of reptiles used for smelling the animals it hunts

lethal — likely to cause death

merges — blends into something else

mound — raised earth, usually round

myth — a story, often very old, usually told to explain an event

paralyze — to make it impossible to move

pit organ — a hollow chamber inside a snake's mouth that allows it to smell out the animals it hunts

plantations — huge farms planted in just a few crops

poisonous — having a deadly substance, such as venom, that causes illness or death

prey — an animal hunted for food

scars — permanent marks of an injury

sheaths — sacs or bags

tadpoles — very young frogs or toads; they have gills, long tail fins, and no legs

termite — a small insect that eats wood and lives with other termites in large nests, or mounds

toxic — poisonous

toxins — poisonous substances often found in venom

tree-dwelling — living in trees

unconscious — unable to awaken but not asleep

venom — a poison made by an animal

visible — able to be seen

Zululand — an area in Northeast Natal, part of the Republic of South Africa

For More Information

Books

I Wonder Why Snakes Shed Their Skin: and Other Questions About Reptiles. I Wonder Why (series). Amanda O'Neill (Kingfisher)

Snake Dictionary: An A to Z of Amazing Snakes. Clint Twist (Tangerine Press)

Snakes. David T. Greenberg (Megan Tingley)

Snakes! Face-to-Face. Jane Hammerslough (Scholastic Paperbacks)

The Best Book of Snakes. Best Book of (series). Christiane Gunzi (Kingfisher)

The Snake Book. Mary Ling and Mary Atkinson (DK Children's)

Web Sites

Kids' Planet: Snakes
www.kidsplanet.org/factsheets/snakes.html

Kids' Turn Central
www.kidsturncentral.com/links/snakelinks.htm

Poisonous Snakes
library.thinkquest.org/5409/specificsnakes.html

San Diego Natural History Museum
www.sdnhm.org/exhibits/reptiles/index.html

Snakes
www.42explore.com/snake.htm

West Central Four Kids Links to Reptiles
www.wc4.org/reptiles_snakes.htm

Index